GW00367935

THE LIFE & TIMES OF

Napoleon Bonaparte

BY
J. Anderson Black

This edition first published by Parragon Books

Produced by
Magpie Books Ltd
7 Kensington Church Court
London W8 4SP

Copyright © Parragon Book Service Ltd 1994

Illustrations courtesy of: Mary Evans Picture Library;
Christies Images.

ISBN 1 85813 932 5

A copy of the British Library Cataloguing in Publication
Data is available from the British Library.

Typeset by Hewer Text Composition Services, Edinburgh
Printed in Singapore by Printlink International Co.

NAPOLEON BONAPARTE

History's most famous Frenchman was not in fact French. He was born, in Ajaccio, Corsica, on 15 August 1769 and christened Napoleone Buonaparte. The island of his birth had been ceded to France a year earlier by the Genoese and this accident of history alone made Napoleon a French subject.

Napoleon was the second surviving child of Carlo and Letizia Buonaparte. His father's family had emigrated to Corsica from Tus-

I

cany in the sixteenth century and, while boasting noble blood, were in fact solidly upper-middle class, a family of judges, civil servants and clergymen. Carlo Buonaparte himself graduated in law from the University of Pisa and then returned to fight for Corsican independence from Genoa. He was something of an opportunist, however, because as soon as the French had established themselves on the island, he abandoned his nationalist principles and entered the services of the new governor, the Count de Marbeuf. Charming and astute, Carlo soon gained political influence in his own right, was accepted into the French aristocracy as a count, and by the time of his death in 1785, at the age of thirty-nine, he was known at the court of King Louis XVI.

One of the perquisites of Carlo's rank was that all his children were granted bursaries to French schools. In 1778, nine-year-old Napoleon and his ten-year-old brother Joseph were enrolled at the Oratorian College at Autun. Joseph studied for the clergy – a vocation which he later abandoned for law – and Napoleon studied French. After three months at Autun, Napoleon won a scholarship to the Royal Military Academy at Brienne. His first months at the academy were a nightmare. He was teased and bullied unmercifully by his fellow students. They ridiculed his strange name, his foreign accent and his diminutive stature. Napoleon took solace in his studies. His endeavours paid off and, in 1784, at the age of fourteen, he won a place at the prestigious *Ecole Militaire* in Paris. This was no mean achievement because the school – the French equivalent of Sandhurst

3

– was reserved mainly for the sons of high nobility. He graduated without great distinction two years later, and was commissioned a second lieutenant of artillery in the regiment of La Fere, garrisoned at Valence. This was an unpromising start to his military career. Future high-flyers almost always came from the cavalry or the infantry.

Napoleon spent the next six years as an impoverished lieutenant. Without the private income enjoyed by the majority of his fellow officers, he had no social life to speak of and spent most of his time at the garrison reading and studying. His tastes were catholic. He developed a passion for military history but also enjoyed the classics, French drama, and the philosophical works of Montesquieu and Rousseau.

THE REVOLUTION

The French Revolution started while Napoleon's regiment was in Auxonne. Like many of his fellow officers, particularly those from more humble backgrounds, he approved of the Revolution in principle. His literary mentors had convinced him that the traditional institutions – the Church, the monarchy and the nobility – were corrupt and inefficient, and that a new order must be created for the nation and its people to achieve their full potential. He also

5

had a more self-serving reason for supporting the Revolution. It promised untold opportunities for talented and ambitious young men like himself who had not inherited positions of power by right of birth.

Napoleon's taste for the Revolution was, however, selective. He had little liking for the principle of popular sovereignty and deplored the public disorder and crowd violence he witnessed during the early days of the insurrection. He perceived the threat of total anarchy when he visited Paris on 10 August 1792 and witnessed the second storming of the Tuileries and the arrest of Louis XVI. In the aftermath of the attack, he was particularly horrified by the spectacle of Parisian market women mutilating the corpses of the Swiss Guards.

From that moment on, Napoleon came to despise and fear the common people of France.

TOULON

Napoleon spent eighteen months, from 1790
to 1791, back in his homeland of Corsica,
helping to consolidate French rule on the
island. Here he had rank and influence, but
he soon tired of things provincial and, in
1793, he decided to rejoin his regiment in
Italy. *En route* he passed close to the port of
Toulon, a major naval base which had
rebelled against the Revolutionary regime
in Paris and was offering safe haven to the
British and Spanish navies. When orders

came down from Paris to besiege Toulon, Napoleon saw his chance for glory. Despite his modest rank, he was given command of an artillery section and set about planning the siege. It was at Toulon that Napoleon first demonstrated his genius both as a strategist and as a leader of men. The siege was an unqualified success. In a little over three days, Napoleon and his artillery bombarded the city into submission, gained control of the harbour and forced the enemy fleets to evacuate. His reward was a meteoric promotion to the rank of brigadier-general and an appointment as commander of planning for the Army of Italy. He was just twenty-four.

He remained in Italy until 1795 when he was re-called to Paris, where mobs under royalist leadership were preparing to storm the Tuileries, the seat of government. Paul

Barras, who was responsible for the defence of the palace, appointed Napoleon his second in command. Napoleon had his men seize forty cannon from the Paris National Guard and position them around the perimeter of the Tuileries. On 5 October, the threatened attack finally materialized and the Parisian masses marched on the palace. When they came within point-blank range of the guns, Napoleon ordered his men to open fire. The crowd was decimated; hundreds died and countless more were injured.

Napoleon's legendary 'whiff of grape shot' established him as a hero of the Revolution and provided him with an entrée to Paris society. He was a guest at the salon of Madame Tallien when he first met Josephine de Beauharnais, a beautiful, aristocratic Creole, widow of General Alexandre de Beauharnais who had been executed during the 'Great Terror' of 1794. It was an unlikely match. At thirty-two, Josephine was six years older than Napoleon, had two teenage children, and was also reputed to have had countless lovers, among them Paul Barras, now a member of the new government, the Directory. Napoleon, however, was dazzled by her beauty and sophistication and proposed marriage. Josephine's past may have been colourful but she was not without influence. It is no coincidence that, two days after the wedding, on 9 March 1796, Napoleon Bonaparte was given the command of the Army of Italy.

The guillotine in the Place de la Revolution

The storming of the Bastille

THE ITALIAN CAMPAIGN

Napoleon left for his new posting with high hopes. During his period as commander of planning for the Army of Italy, he had spent much of his time and energy devising an elaborate strategy for the invasion and conquest of the Italian peninsula, much of which was occupied by the Austrians. Now was his chance to put it to the test. When he arrived at the army headquarters at Savona, however, he found his army, which on paper consisted of 43,000 men, in fact numbered scarcely 30,000; and even these were ill-fed, ill-equipped, untrained and dispirited. Napoleon once again demonstrated his extraordinary charisma and leadership. He addressed his ragtag army in an inspirational tone: 'Soldiers, you are naked, badly fed . . . Rich provinces and great towns will be within your power, and in them you will find honour, glory and wealth. Soldiers of Italy, will you be wanting in courage and steadfastness?'

And it was not just words. Napoleon secured loans in Genoa and equipped his men in a manner befitting a modern fighting force. On 12 April, barely a month after taking command, Napoleon marched his army south. He had a string of swift and spectacular victories at Matenotte, Dego, Millesimo and Mondovi, defeating the Austrian and

Sardinian armies, and then took Turin. The Austrian army continued to retreat as Napoleon took Milan and drove on towards Mantua. Here, in the great fortress city, the Austrians had consolidated their army and Napoleon met the first serious opposition of his Italian campaign. As the battle for control of Mantua dragged on, Napoleon signed peace agreements with the King of Sardinia, the dukes of Parma and Modena, and Pope Pius VI.

Mantua finally capitulated in February 1797 and Napoleon, against orders from the Directory in Paris, marched his army across the Alps on Vienna. By the middle of April, he was within fifty miles of the capital, but the Austrians sued for an armistice before a shot was fired.

Napoleon returned to Paris in triumph. Still only twenty-eight years old, he had established himself as the most famous general in France. He was elected to the prestigious Institut, an honour which he coveted. There he flattered the scholars and intellectuals by telling them, 'the greatest conquests are those made against ignorance.'

Not everyone was pleased to have Napoleon back in Paris, however. Some members of the Directory were already deeply suspicious of his motives. Napoleon was by now an overtly political animal and he was perceived as a potential threat to the stability of the government.

EGYPT

Napoleon's campaign had secured peace in mainland Europe after five years of conflict, but the war at sea with the British continued. The Directory, who wanted to launch an invasion of the British Isles, had little choice but to offer Napoleon command of the army which was assembled along the Channel coast in readiness for the attack. Napoleon reviewed the situation and came to the conclusion that the invasion was doomed to failure unless and until France had command of the sea. Instead he suggested a rearguard action, to attack Britain's resources by occupying Egypt and cutting off her trade routes with India and the Far East. This plan was approved by the Directory as much to get the ambitious young general out of the way as for any strategic consideration.

Napoleon's campaign began well. On 10 June 1798 his forces occupied the island fortress of Malta; three weeks later they stormed into Alexandria, and within a matter of days the entire Nile Delta was in French hands. On 1 August, however, Napoleon suffered a serious set-back when his entire fleet was destroyed in the Battle of the Nile by the British Navy, commanded by Admiral Horatio Nelson.

Without ships, Napoleon found himself marooned in the very territory that he had just conquered. And the Turks, who had nominal suzerainty over Egypt, were incensed by Napoleon's antics. They allied themselves with the British and the Russians, and declared war on France.

Anticipating an attack from Turkey, Napoleon marched his army north-east into Syria, but at Acre he suffered the second major military defeat of his career, this time at the hands of British and Turkish forces. He had no choice but to retreat into Egypt. There he handed over his command to General Jean Baptiste Kleber and sailed for France.

THE COUP

Napoleon reached Paris on 14 October 1799 to find that France, in his absence, had lost control of most of the territories he had won for her in Italy, and the Directory was in a state of chaos. Napoleon Bonaparte, still only thirty years old, was widely seen as France's best hope of salvation. He was approached by two of the Directors, Talleyrand and Sieyes, with a plan to overthrow the government. They needed Napoleon to take command of the army and support their coup.

BONAPARTE 1ᵉ Consul.

Napoleon as First Consul

Josephine

The *coup d'état* was executed on 10 November 1799. Directors were forced to resign; the Directory was abolished, and a new government, a consulate, was established. Three consuls were appointed: Napoleon, Sieyes and Roger-Ducos. The three men were nominally equal, but it did not take First Consul Bonaparte long to outmanoeuvre Sieyes and Roger-Ducos and establish himself as *de facto* dictator of France.

The French people soon learned that Napoleon was not only a brilliant general, he was an enormously gifted statesman and administrator. He set up a strong central government and appointed prefects to head the territorial areas. He reorganized the education system, and founded the Imperial University. His government revised the laws of France so effectively that the *Code Napoleon* remains the basis of French law to this day. In 1800, he established the Bank of France, and poured money into the Louvre, the *Bibliotheque Nationale* and other cultural institutions. The following year, he drew up a treaty with the Pope, clarifying the confused relations which had existed between Church and State since the Revolution. He also negotiated peace treaties with his old rivals the Austrians and the British.

THE EMPEROR

In 1802, Napoleon was voted consul for life, but he had grander plans for himself and his family. He wanted to establish a hereditary monarchy with himself at the head. To this end he purged the capital of die-hard republicans, several of whom were executed, and packed the Senate with his own supporters.

In May 1804, he got his way when the Senate proclaimed Napoleon Bonaparte 'Emperor of the French'. A popular vote supported this decision by 3,572,329 to 2,579. He was crowned in Notre–Dame Cathedral on 2 December 1804.

In 1803, the British, alarmed by Napoleon's aggression and publicly stated expansionist ambitions, declared war on France again. It was a conflict which neither side could expect to win with ease. Napoleon knew that his only hope of victory was to land an army on British soil; while the British could only defeat Napoleon by forming a continental alliance against him.

A successful invasion of Britain, as Napoleon had stated in 1798, was dependent upon France establishing sea supremacy. He gathered a fleet of nearly 2000 ships in the Channel ports between Brest and Antwerp and, at the same time, assembled his *Grande*

Armee at Boulogne. Even with his considerable navy, however, Napoleon knew that he could not hope to defeat the British at sea unless he enlisted the help of the Spanish.

Spain, hoping to ride on Napoleon's coattails, declared war on Britain in December 1804. The Spanish and French fleets then agreed to mass in the Antilles, hoping to lure a British squadron into those waters. The plan turned into a fiasco. The Spanish never turned up, and Admiral Pierre de Villeneuve, finding himself alone and faced with the might of Nelson's fleet, turned back to Europe. His fleet took refuge in Cadiz on 18 July 1805, where the British blockaded it. Napoleon was enraged by this humiliation, accused de Villeneuve of cowardice and ordered him to run the blockade, join the Spanish squadron and make for Toulon. The

French fleet set sail but, on 21 October 1805, they were attacked by Nelson off Cape Trafalgar and the Franco-Spanish fleet was totally destroyed. All ideas of an invasion of Britain were thus abandoned.

Napoleon found other uses for his *Grande Armee*, however. He attacked and defeated the Austrians at Ulm, and then went on to defeat the combined armies of Russia and Austria at the Battle of Austerlitz on 13 November 1805. This was arguably the greatest military victory of Napoleon's career. In the peace treaty which followed the battle, the Austrians were obliged to renounce all claims to their Italian territories together with their extensive holdings in Germany. Napoleon then assumed the crown of Italy and installed Josephine's son, Eugene de Beauharnais, as his viceroy.

Napoleon in Egypt

Emperor of France and King of Italy

Next he dethroned the Bourbons from the Kingdom of Naples and bestowed the crown on his older brother, Joseph. His younger brother, Louis, was installed as King of Holland. He made himself protector of the Swiss and German confederations.

Just when it seemed that no one would stand against Napoleon's France, Prussia, backed by the Russians, declared war. It turned out to be a hopeless mismatch. With lightning thrusts, Napoleon demolished the fabled Prussian army at the battles of Jena and Auerstadt (October 1806) and then went on to defeat the Russians at Friedland in June of the following year. In the aftermath of these victories, he created the kingdom of Westphalia and installed yet another of his brothers, Jerome.

THE ZENITH

Since the invasion of Britain was unrealistic, Napoleon decided to induce her capitulation by crippling her economy. In 1806, he announced a blockade of British ports, a plan which he dubbed the 'Continental System'. This forbade all trade with the British Isles, ordered the confiscation of all goods leaving Britain or attempting to land there, and condemned as fair prize any ship which touched the coasts of Britain or its colonies. Of all the major European powers only the Portuguese resisted the Continental System. Not only were they Britain's oldest ally, but they also faced economic ruin if trade between the two countries was interrupted.

In 1807, Napoleon responded to this act of defiance by marching on Lisbon and, while he was at it, seized control of his erstwhile ally, Spain. He installed his brother Joseph on the throne of Spain, and gave Naples to his sister Caroline and her husband, Marshal Joachim Murat. Spain would not accept Joseph, however, and rebelled. Napoleon had to go there personally, together with 300,000 troops, to consolidate his brother's sovereignty. After his departure, however, the civil war resumed and, aided by an Anglo-Portuguese army, the Spaniards fought to regain control of their country.

The war continued for almost four years, badly damaging Napoleon's colonial aspirations, until Joseph was finally expelled in 1813. 'That miserable Spanish affair', Napoleon said much later, 'was what killed me.'

Meanwhile, in 1809, Napoleon defeated the Austrians again. His empire was now at its zenith and he saw and spoke of himself as Charlemagne's rightful heir. Only one problem remained. For his vision of a dynasty to become a reality, he needed a legitimate heir. Josephine, now forty-five, was unable to provide him with one, so he divorced her and married Archduchess Marie-Louise, an eighteen-year-old beauty and daughter of the Austrian Emperor, Francis I. There is no doubt that the marriage had a political dimension, but, against all odds, it turned out to be a true love-match. It also produced the son that Napoleon craved, a child who was given the title King of Rome before he was even born.

Napoleon's empire was now at its most far-reaching and included the Illyrian provinces, Etruria, some of the Papal States, Holland and the German states bordering the North Sea. Around the empire proper was a ring of states ruled over by Napoleon's relatives: the kingdom of Westphalia (Jerome Bonaparte); the kingdom of Spain (Joseph Bonaparte); the kingdom of Italy (Eugene de Beauharnais); the kingdom of Holland (Louis Bonaparte); the kingdom of Naples (Joachim Murat); and the principality of Lucca and Piombino (Felix Baciocchi, Napoleon's brother-in-law). Then there were other territories closely bound to France by treaties: the Swiss Confederation, of which Napoleon was mediator; the Confederation of the Rhine; the duchy of Warsaw; and even Austria seemed bound to France by Napoleon's marriage to Marie-Louise.

'I am building a family of kings', Napoleon boasted to Miot, Count de Melito, '. . . or rather of viceroys.' Unfortunately for Napoleon, ambition appears to have been a family trait, and several of his relatives became dissatisfied with pro-consular roles. Joseph, in Spain, had ambitions to become a constitutional monarch. He protested against French atrocities in *his* country, and generally showed more interest in social reforms than he did in his brother's grand design. In Holland, his brother Louis refused to institute the *Code Napoleon* which he considered 'unDutch'; and in Westphalia, Jerome sided with his parliament against Napoleon's relentless demands for money and troops.

Napoleon was becoming disenchanted with his own family whom he had given positions of power specifically as a hedge against treachery. He now preferred professional pro-consuls like Camille de Tournon, prefect of Rome, who ruled with an iron fist, kept the peace and produced handsome revenues for the French exchequer.

The truth of the situation is that Napoleon was now in the grips of full-blown megalomania. In 1809, he had seized the Papal States, and the following year had proclaimed Rome the 'Second City of the Empire'. He wrote to Pope Pius VII: 'We return to the times of Charlemagne', and offered him the title of imperial chaplain.

Much to Napoleon's chagrin, Pius declined the offer.

In 1810, Napoleon decided that it was time his own family were brought to task. He forced Louis to abdicate his throne and annexed Holland to France. In Spain, Joseph was relegated to Governor of Madrid. Murat and Jerome were subjected to much the same treatment, as Napoleon imposed a system of central government from Paris.

DISASTER IN RUSSIA

On 31 December 1810, the Russians announced that they were no longer prepared to observe the Continental System and intended to resume trade with Britain. Napoleon responded by assembling a massive army on the Russian border in Poland. The force, which amounted to some 600,000 men, was drawn from every region of the empire, and outnumbered the Russian army by almost three to one. Napoleon attempted to negotiate with the Tsar from this position of strength but the talks broke down and, on 29 June 1812, the *Grande Armee* crossed the Neiman into Russia. The Russians retreated, scorching the earth behind them.

The two armies finally engaged at Borodino, near Moscow, on 7 September 1812. Despite the numerical disparity, General Mikhail Kutuzov's forces matched the French in a bloody but indecisive battle. The Russians retreated to Moscow and the French regrouped. A week later, on 14 September, Napoleon finally led his troops into the capital, only to find that it had been abandoned under cover of darkness by Kutuzov and his forces. Later that same day, a massive fire broke out which almost totally destroyed the city and, along with it, the supplies it had promised. Napoleon had no choice but to withdraw.

Napoleon and staff in the Place de la Concorde

Admiral Nelson boards a French ship

The Russian winter achieved what no enemy force had ever done. It annihilated
Napoleon's forces. By the time it re-crossed
the Neiman in November 1812, the piercing
cold and hunger had reduced the *Grande
Armee* from a fighting force of more than half
a million men to less than 10,000.

THE BEGINNING
OF THE END

News of the Russian catastrophe spread through Europe and people finally began to believe that they could resist Napoleon's will. In Germany there was an outbreak of anti-French demonstrations; the Prussian troops deserted the *Grande Armee* and turned against the French; and in Italy there was a move away from Napoleon as patriots looked to Eugene de Beauharnais and Murat for the unification of the peninsula.

Even in France itself there were signs of discontent. During Napoleon's retreat from Moscow there had been an unsuccessful *coup d'état*. But Napoleon was not about to relinquish his hold over France or his empire. When he finally returned to Paris on 18 December 1812, he set about ousting the malcontents from the Senate, strengthening the dictatorship, raising funds and building himself a new army.

So, in 1813, Napoleon and France found themselves on the defensive for the first time in almost twenty years. The emperor's depleted forces were lined up against the armies of nations fighting for their freedom, and the French themselves no longer had the stomach for war. Napoleon's ambitions no longer reflected the mood of the nation.

He did have a measure of success against the Russians and Prussians at the battles of Lutzen and Bautzen, but his army was in need of reorganization and reinforcement. He could not hope to defend France, let alone protect the empire, and so, when the Austrians joined the fray in the role of armed mediators, Napoleon reluctantly agreed to an armistice.

Austria, as arbiter, proved generous and fair in the conditions they proposed to the beleaguered emperor: the French empire was to return to its pre-imperial borders; the duchy of Warsaw and the Confederation of the Rhine were to be dissolved; and Prussia would be defined by its frontiers of 1805. Napoleon would have been wise to accept the deal but he prevaricated, and the Austrians, their patience exhausted, declared war on France.

Napoleon goes into battle

Empress Marie-Louise

The French now found themselves in a truly hopeless situation. The numerical superiority of the enemy armies was increasing by the day as one German contingent after another defected to the allies. But Napoleon was still not prepared to admit defeat. He finally met the combined armies of his enemies at Leipzig on 16 October 1813 in what became known as the 'Battle of the Nations'. In three days of fierce fighting, Napoleon's *Grande Armee* was torn to ribbons.

Throughout the empire, one disaster followed another. In Spain, the French army had been forced to retreat and had then been defeated at the Battle of Vittoria. In the Pyrenees, the British were threatening France's southern defences; in Italy, the Austrians took control of Romagna; and in Naples,

Murat betrayed his patron and defected to Austria.

By January 1814, France was under attack on all frontiers. The allies pulled off a propaganda coup when they announced that their fight was not against the French people, but against Napoleon, for it had been he alone who had refused the conditions offered by the Austrian arbiters, whereby France would have retained her original integrity. Sympathy for Napoleon was ebbing fast.

He did have one final flurry in the spring of 1814 and achieved truly astonishing results with a small army of young conscripts, but even he must have realised that the situation was ultimately hopeless.

On 9 March 1814, Austria, Britain, Russia and Prussia signed the Treaty of Chaumont in which the four nations formed an alliance for twenty years, agreed not to negotiate individually with France, and promised to continue the fight until Napoleon was overthrown. They then mustered their armies and marched on Paris.

By the time the allies reached the gates of the capital, on 30 March, Napoleon had moved his army east with the intention of attacking their rearguard. The Parisian authorities, by now thoroughly disenchanted with their emperor, quickly came to terms with the allies. A new government was formed under the leadership of Talleyrand who, without consulting the electorate, announced the deposition of Napoleon and the reinstatement of the Bourbon monarchy in the person of Louis XVIII.

News of the Senate's capitulation reached Napoleon at Vitre. He immediately ordered his army to move west towards Paris. He and he alone wanted to fight on. When the army reached Fontainebleau on 4 April, his marshals pleaded with him to stop. The troops, they insisted, were tired, demoralised and vastly outnumbered; the battle was lost. Marshal Ney ended the meeting by suggesting that Napoleon abdicate. At first the emperor steadfastly refused to consider this suggestion, but the following day he learned that General Marmont, commander of his vanguard, had defected with his entire corps. Two days later, on 6 April 1814, Napoleon Bonaparte announced his abdication.

The Treaty of Fontainebleau was signed five days later, under whose terms Napoleon was assigned sovereignty over the Mediterranean island of Elba. He was allowed to take a personal guard of 400 men with him, was granted a personal income of 2,000,000 francs per annum, and was permitted to continue to use the title of emperor. After an unsuccessful attempt at poisoning himself, Napoleon finally agreed to the allies's conditions and departed for Elba.

THE HUNDRED DAYS

Napoleon's new empire was an island measuring less than twenty-five square miles. It was a far cry from his dreams of outstripping Charlemagne, but he feigned contentment. 'I want from now on', he declared, 'to live like a justice of the peace.'

Napoleon was still only forty-five years old and one suspects that he had absolutely no intention of drifting into docile retirement. He was merely biding his time.

Napoleon leaves Fontainebleau for Elba

Napoleon crosses the Alps

He was kept abreast of developments in Paris, where the Bourbon restoration was already in trouble. True, the people of France had tired of the emperor, but they had not lost sight of the achievements and values of the Revolution, and they certainly had not approved the restoration of the monarchy. Everything Louis XVIII stood for was an anathema to them, and it was not long before conspiracies were being hatched against the crown.

In Elba, Napoleon had abandoned any pretence of contentment. He had not received his promised allowance and he was convinced that the Austrians were preventing Marie-Louise and his son from travelling to the island. In reality she had taken a lover and had no intention of joining him.

His own situation, combined with the French people's disenchantment with the status quo, galvanized Napoleon into action. In February 1815, he sailed for France with a detachment of his guard. On 1 March, the 'thunderer of the scene' (Lord Byron's description) landed at Antibes and marched towards Paris. As he crossed the Alps, the republican peasantry rallied round him. Thenceforth 'the eagle flew from steeple to steeple until it reached Notre-Dame.'

On 20 March 1815, Napoleon marched into Paris to a tumultuous welcome. Louis XVIII had fled.

Napoleon was reinstated head of state, not so much as a mark of his imperial achievements, but more as an embodiment of the spirit of the Revolution. His return, of course, did not go unnoticed by the allied forces, who began to mass on France's borders. Napoleon's reaction to this was typical. He mustered an army, marched into Belgium and, on 16 June 1815, confronted and defeated the Prussian army under General Gebhard von Blucher at the Battle of Ligny. Two days later, however, it was a different story. At Waterloo, he met the British forces commanded by Wellington. Napoleon attacked frontally, with none of his customary finesse. Despite this, his army was in sight of victory when von Blucher and the remnants of the Prussian forces arrived to reinforce the British. The French were defeated by the sheer force of numbers. Napoleon had fought his last battle.

ST HELENA

Back in Paris, Napoleon was forced to abdicate for a second time. He did so in favour of his illegitimate son, Napoleon II, on 22 June 1815. He arrived at Rochefort ten days later and prepared to set sail for the United States, but the British had blockaded the port and he was stranded. Napoleon decided to appeal to the British for protection. He wrote to the Prince Regent, later King George IV:

Royal Highness,

A prey to the factions which divide my
country and to the hostility of the greatest
powers in Europe, I have ended my political
career and I am going, like Themistocles, to
seat myself at the hearth of the British people.
I put myself under the protection of its laws,
which I ask from your Royal Highness, as
from the most powerful, the most constant,
and the most generous of my enemies.

As Napoleon waited for a reply in Rochefort, the allies argued about what should be
done with the deposed emperor. They were
agreed on one point: he should not be
allowed to return to Elba. Nor did they
like the idea of his going to the United
States. He had to be placed somewhere
inaccessible, where there was no audience
for his rallying calls. They decided on

St Helena, a rocky island in the South Atlantic, a thousand miles off the West African coast. Napoleon could not do much damage there.

News of the decision reached Napoleon via Captain F.L. Maitland, master of the *Bellerophon*, one of the blockading British ships. Napoleon's reaction was simple and eloquent: 'I appeal to history'.

Napoleon sailed to Plymouth aboard the *Bellerophon* and was transferred to the *Northumberland*, which set sail on 10 August 1815. She anchored off St Helena on Sunday, 15 October 1815, and Napoleon was put ashore, along with a small retinue of supporters who had followed him voluntarily into exile. They included General Bertrand, grand marshal of the palace; General Month-

Napoleon greeted on his return from Elba

Emperor of France

olon, aide-de-camp; Las Cases, former chamberlain; and a collection of servants, including Napoleon's personal valet, Louis Marchand. They were all housed in a building called the Briars, the property of an Englishman, William Balcome, while the main house on the island, the magnificent Longwood House, was being restored in readiness for the emperor.

It is fair to assume that, from this time on, Napoleon lapsed into a deeper and deeper depression. He was free to go wherever he wanted on the island, so long as he was accompanied by a British officer, but he seldom took advantage of this liberty. He settled into a routine, rising at 10 a.m. and spending his days within Longwood House and its environs. He wrote a little. Las Cases acted as secretary as Napoleon dictated notes

for a book which was published in 1823
under the title of *Memorial de Sainte-Helene*.
He dined from 7 p.m. to 8 p.m., after which
Las Cases would read the classics to him. The
latter part of the evening was spent playing
cards and, at around midnight, Napoleon
would retire.

It was not long before Napoleon's health
started to deteriorate. This was certainly not
caused by his living conditions. St Helena had
a wonderful climate and food was fresh and
plentiful. The problem lay in the very inac-
tivity to which he was subjected. He was the
ultimate man of action, a man who had been at
the centre of world politics for twenty years,
who had fought and defeated the great armies
of Europe. The monotony of his existence on
this little island, aggravated by his self-imposed
isolation, must have been intolerable. And

there was another, more personal, cause for his misery and depression. He was still deeply in love with his wife, Marie-Louise. He had had no word from her, and it is probable that he had learned of her affair with Graff A. A. von Neipperg. (She subsequently married von Neipperg without waiting for Napoleon's death.) Nor had he heard from his son, the former king of Rome, who was now living in Vienna under the title of the Duke of Reichstadt.

And then there was Sir Hudson Lowe, the Governor of St Helena – in effect, Napoleon's jailer. Napoleon disliked the man on principle. He had been commander of the Corsican rangers, a band of mercenaries recruited by the British, most of whom were avowed enemies of the Bonaparte family. Lowe was a fastidious, fussy man, obsessed with carrying out his orders in precise detail. He came into conflict with Las Cases, whom he considered a disruptive influence on the island, and had him arrested and expelled. This was a terrible blow to Napoleon, who had come to see Las Cases as his only true companion.

It was shortly after Las Cases left St Helena, in the winter of 1817, that Napoleon showed the first signs of severe illness. He suffered from terrible stomach pains, which have subsequently been diagnosed as either ulcers or stomach cancer (his father had died of stomach cancer at the age of thirty-nine). The island's doctor, a cheery Irishman called Barry O'Meara, pleaded with Lowe that his patient should be allowed to leave St Helena to receive proper treatment. Lowe flatly refused this request and dismissed

The Duke of Wellington

Napoleon's house on St Helena

O'Meara. The same fate awaited his successor, Dr John Stokie, who was well disposed towards Napoleon. Lowe replaced Stokie with an undistinguished but pliant Corsican physician, Dr C.F. Antommarchi. Antommarchi did his best, but he was clearly out of his depth. In any case, it is doubtful whether Napoleon would have survived, regardless of the treatment administered to him.

By March 1821 Napoleon was bedridden, and the following month he dictated his last will and testament: 'I wish my ashes to rest on the banks of the Seine, in the midst of the French people I have loved so much. I die before my time, killed by the English oligarchy and its hired assassins . . .'

At 5.49 p.m. on 5 May 1821, Napoleon Bonaparte died. He was fifty-one years old.

Permission for his body to be returned to Paris for burial was refused and so, dressed in his favourite uniform, that of the *Chasseurs de la Garde*, and draped in a grey overcoat he had worn at the Battle of Morengo, he was buried on the island of St Helena. The headstone of his grave bore no name, only the words 'Ci-git' ('Here lies').

In 1840, in a wave of pro-Napoleon sentiment, the French government finally relented and had his remains exhumed, shipped to Paris, and interred in a tomb under the dome of the *Hotel des Invalides*, a hospital for French war veterans. A century later, the body of Napoleon's only legitimate son, the king of Rome and Duke of Reichstat, who died in 1832, was moved from his grave in Vienna, on the orders of Adolf Hitler, to lie beside his father.

THE LEGACY

The failure of the hundred day campaign and Napoleon's subsequent exile spawned a torrent of books designed to sully the emperor's reputation. This hostility soon died down, however, and it became fashionable to defend his record. This mood is exemplified in Byron's 'Ode to Napoleon', and Stendhal's *Vie de Napoleon*. And the Napoleonic legend has persisted from that time to the present day, inspiring novelists, poets and playwrights from Victor Hugo to Andre

Malraux; and musicians from Beethoven to
Prokoviev.

How does history view him today? At one
end of the scale he is seen as the 'Corsican
ogre', a man who sacrificed the lives of one-
sixth of the population of France for his
ambitions. At the other he is considered a
military genius and architect of modern
France. There are elements of truth in both
arguments. He both fulfilled and distorted
the legacy of the French Revolution, reject-
ing the concept of popular politics, but
preserving equality before the law for ordin-
ary people. However, it is certainly hard to
reconcile press censorship and the restoration
of slavery in the colonies with the principles
of the Revolution. On the other hand, at
home, Napoleon stood by the ideal of
religious tolerance; his treatment of the Jews

would put many later European rulers to shame.

As for the argument that Napoleon was the architect of modern France, again this is open to debate. The fact is that the social structure of France changed very little under the empire. It remained roughly what the Revolution had made it. Three in four of the population were peasants. Half of them worked their own land; the other half hired out their labour. Industry certainly flourished during the empire period, but this was largely fuelled by Napoleon's own military requirement, and it certainly did not outstrip that of the other major European nations during the early nineteenth century.

Napoleon's abiding and indisputable legacy was the establishment of durable institutions:

the administrative system; the *Code Napoleon*, which forms the basis of modern French law; the judicial system; the *Banque de France*, the universities and military academies; the libraries, museums and galleries. They all stand today, a tangible testament to a man of colossal imagination, ambition and vigour.

H. A. L. Fisher summed up the enigma which is Napoleon seventy years ago: 'Never was so brilliant a twin fugue upon the twin themes of patriotism and glory addressed to the multitude of any country.'

CHRONOLOGY

1769

15 August, Napoleon born at Ajaccio, Corsica, the second son of Carlo and Letizia Buonaparte.

1779

April, Napoleon enters the Military Academy at Brienne.

1784

October, Napoleon transfers to the *Ecole Militaire* in Paris.

1785

September, Napoleon graduates from the *Ecole Militaire*. He is commissioned second lieutenant of artillery and is garrisoned at Valence.

1790

Napoleon returns to Corsica to help consolidate French rule.

1792

Napoleon rejoins his regiment in France. 10 August, Napoleon witnesses the second storming of the Tuileries in Paris.

1793

September, Napoleon commands the artillery at the siege of Toulon, his first military victory. He is promoted to the rank of brigadier-general.

1795

October, Napoleon supports Barras in the suppression of the royalist uprising in Paris.

1796

March, Napoleon marries Josephine de Beauharnais. He is given command of the French Army in Italy.

May, French victories at Matenotte, Dego, Millesimo, Mondovi and Lodi. Napoleon takes Milan.

August, French victory at Castiglione.

October, French victory at Arcola.

1797

February, Napoleon takes control of Mantua.

April, Napoleon negotiates armistice with Austria.

May, Napoleon returns to Paris a national hero.

1798
May, Napoleon sets sail for Egypt.

June, French occupy Malta.

July, Battle of the Nile. French gain control of the Nile Delta.

August, Napoleon's fleet destroyed by Nelson at Aboukir Bay.

1799
February, French defeated at the Battle of Acre. Napoleon retreats to Egypt.

July, French victory over the Turks at Aboukir.

August, Napoleon leaves for France.

November, *coup d'état* of Brumiere. The Directory of France is abolished and replaced by a senate. Napoleon is elected First Consul and *de facto* ruler of France.

1800
Napoleon reforms local and national government, education and legislature.

1801
July, Concordat with the Pope.

1802
August, Napoleon confirmed by plebiscite as consul for life.

1803

May, outbreak of war between France and Britain.

December, the *Grande Armee* assembled at Boulogne in readiness to invade Britain.

1804

May, the Senate proclaims Napoleon 'Emperor of the French'.

December, Napoleon's coronation at Notre-Dame. Spain forms an alliance with France and declares war on Britain.

1805

August, Napoleon invades Germany.

October, French victory at Ulm, defeat at Trafalgar.

November, French victory at Austerlitz. Napoleon crowned king of Italy. Joseph Bonaparte made king of Naples. Louis Bonaparte becomes king of Holland.

1806
July, creation of the Confederation of the Rhine.

September, Prussia declares war on France.

October, French victories over Prussians at Jena and Auerstadt.

November, introduction of the Continental System.

1807
June, French victory over the Russians at the Battle of Friedland.

July, creation of the Grand Duchy of Warsaw.

November, Lisbon occupied by French forces.

1808
May, Charles IV cedes his rights in Spain to Napoleon.

July, Joseph Bonaparte assumes the throne of Spain.

November, Napoleon enters Spain to consolidate his brother's sovereignty.

1809
Britain allies itself with Austria in the war against France.

December, Napoleon divorces Josephine.

1810
April, Napoleon marries Marie-Louise.

July, Holland annexed to France.

November, northern Germany annexed to France.

December, Russia renounces the Continental System.

1811
March, Marie-Louise bears Napoleon a son, titled the King of Rome.

1812
June, French cross the Neimen and start the Russian Campaign.

French defeat in Spain.

September, Battle of Borodino. Napoleon enters Moscow.

October, French retreat from Moscow.

10 November, survivors of the *Grande Armee* re-cross the Neimen.

18 December, Napoleon reaches Paris.

1813
February, the Prussians enter an alliance with Russia against France.

May, French victories at Lutzen and Bautzen.

October, Napoleon defeated at Leipzig in the 'Battle of the Nations'.

December, allied invasion of France.

1814
March, Paris falls to the allies.

April, Napoleon abdicates.

May, Napoleon exiled to the island of Elba.

1815
March, Napoleon returns to France. The beginning of the 'Hundred Days'.

April, Napoleon establishes a new government in Paris.

June, victory at Ligny and defeat at Waterloo.

Napoleon's second abdication.

October, Napoleon arrives in St Helena.

1821
5 May, Napoleon dies.

LIFE AND TIMES

Julius Caesar
Hitler
Monet
Van Gogh
Beethoven
Mozart
Mother Teresa
Florence Nightingale
Anne Frank
Napoleon

LIFE AND TIMES

JFK
Martin Luther King
Marco Polo
Christopher Columbus
Stalin
William Shakespeare
Oscar Wilde
Castro
Gandhi
Einstein